How To Swim With The Sharks Without Being Eaten Alive

Survival Tactics for the Modern Professional

Ann R. Moyers

DISCLAIMER

While every precaution has been taken in the preparation of this book, the publisher assumes no responsibility for errors or omissions, or for damages resulting from the use of the information contained herein.

How To Swim With The Sharks Without Being Eaten Alive: Survival Tactics for the Modern Professional

First edition.

How To Swim With The Sharks Without Being Eaten Alive

COPYRIGHT © ANN R. MOYERS 2024. ALL RIGHTS RESERVED

Before this document can be legally duplicated or reproduced in any manner, the publisher's consent must be gained. Therefore, the contents within this document can neither be stored electronically, transferred, nor kept in a database. Neither in part, nor in full can this document be copied, scanned, faxed, or retained without approval from the publisher or creator.

TABLE OF CONTENTS

Disclaimer 2
Copyright © Ann R. Moyers 2024. All Rights Reserved 3
Table of Contents 4
Introduction 8
    The Sharks Are Out There 8
        Identifying the sharks: Who are they and what do they want? 8
    The predatory mindset: How sharks think and operate 11
Chapter 1 15
    The Shark-Infested Waters 15
        The corporate jungle: Navigating the treacherous workplace 15
    The shark-infested marketplace: Surviving in a competitive world 17
Chapter 2 21
    Shark Bait: Common Mistakes 21
        Avoid becoming prey: Understanding the mistakes that make you vulnerable 21
Chapter 3 26
    The Armor of Confidence 26
        Building self-esteem: Believing in your abilities 26
    Projecting confidence: Communicating assertively 28
Chapter 4 32
    The Art of Deception 32
        Strategic bluffing: Using deception to your advantage . 32

Advanced Negotiation Tactics 34
The Power of Persuasion 38
Reading others: Understanding their intentions 40

Chapter 5 44
The Power of Networking 44
Building alliances: Forming relationships with influential people 44
Leveraging your network: Using connections to your advantage 47

Chapter 6 51
The Predator Becomes the Prey 51
Turning the tables: Taking control of the situation 51
Setting boundaries: Protecting yourself from exploitation 54

Chapter 7 57
The Art of Survival 57
Adapting to change: Embracing uncertainty 57
Maintaining resilience: Bouncing back from setbacks 59
Essential Skills for Self-Defense 62

Chapter 8 66
The Shark's Perspective 66
Thinking like a shark: Adopting a predatory mindset .. 66
Becoming a leader: Inspiring others to follow 68

Chapter 9 72
The Legacy of the Survivor 72
Leaving a lasting impact: Making a difference in the world 72

Embracing the journey: Finding fulfillment in the struggle 74

Conclusion... 77

PART I

Understanding the Sharks

INTRODUCTION
THE SHARKS ARE OUT THERE

IDENTIFYING THE SHARKS: WHO ARE THEY AND WHAT DO THEY WANT?

In the treacherous waters of the corporate world, sharks are everywhere. They're not just the obvious predators, the ruthless bosses and cutthroat competitors, but also the more subtle threats: the backstabbing colleagues, the manipulative office politicians, and the self-serving opportunists. To survive in this environment, it's essential to be able to identify these sharks before they strike.

The Office Predator: This is the most obvious shark. It's the boss who demands unreasonable hours, the coworker who steals your ideas, and the competitor who tries to undermine your success. These predators are often driven by a desire for power, control, or personal gain.

The Office Politician: This shark operates behind the scenes, manipulating others to achieve their own ends. They may spread rumors, form alliances, or sabotage the efforts of others. Office politicians are often motivated by a desire for status, recognition, or advancement.

The Backstabber: This shark is a master of deception. They may appear friendly and supportive, but behind your back, they're spreading rumors and undermining your reputation. Backstabbers are often driven by jealousy, envy, or a desire to get ahead at any cost.

The Opportunist: This shark is always on the lookout for opportunities to advance their own interests. They may be willing to compromise their principles or betray their friends to get ahead. Opportunists are often motivated by greed, ambition, or a lack of loyalty.

The Toxic Coworker: This shark is a negative force in the workplace. They may be constantly complaining, gossiping, or creating drama. Toxic coworkers can make it difficult to focus and be productive.

The Bullies: These sharks use intimidation and aggression to get their way. They may bully others through physical threats, verbal abuse, or social isolation. Bullies are often driven by a desire for power, control, or a need to feel superior.

The Gaslighters: These sharks manipulate others by denying their experiences or making them doubt their own sanity. Gaslighters may make false accusations, twist the truth, or blame others for their own mistakes.

The Narcissists: These sharks are overly self-absorbed and believe they are superior to others. They may exploit others to achieve their own ends. Narcissists are often driven by a need for admiration and attention.

The Psychopaths: These sharks are individuals who lack empathy and remorse. They may be capable of extreme violence or cruelty. Psychopaths are often driven by a desire for power, control, or excitement.

The Passive-Aggressive Sharks: These sharks express their aggression indirectly, often through sarcasm, procrastination, or sabotage. Passive-aggressive sharks may be motivated by resentment, anger, or a desire to avoid confrontation.

The Energy Vampires: These sharks drain the energy of others with their constant negativity and complaining. Energy vampires may be motivated by a desire for attention or a fear of being alone.

The Gatekeepers: These sharks control access to resources or information. They may use their position to limit the opportunities of others. Gatekeepers may be motivated by a desire for power, control, or a fear of losing their influence.

The Microaggressions: These sharks make subtle, often unintentional comments or behaviors that can be harmful or offensive. Microaggressions may be motivated by unconscious biases or stereotypes.

The Ghosters: These sharks suddenly disappear without explanation. They may ghost others to avoid confrontation or because they no longer find them interesting or useful.

The Social Climbers: These sharks are always trying to network with more influential people. They may be willing to compromise their principles or values to get ahead. Social climbers may be motivated by a desire for status, recognition, or power.

The Enablers: These sharks support and encourage the harmful behaviors of others. Enablers may be motivated by fear, guilt, or a desire to maintain their relationships.

The Saboteurs: These sharks intentionally try to ruin the plans or projects of others. Saboteurs may be motivated by jealousy, envy, or a desire to get ahead at any cost.

The Gossip Mongers: These sharks spread rumors and gossip about others. Gossip mongers may be motivated by a desire for attention, a need to feel superior, or a desire to harm others.

The Cliques: These sharks form exclusive groups that exclude others. Cliques may be motivated by a desire for power, control, or a sense of belonging.

The Toxic Teams: These sharks create a negative and hostile work environment. Toxic teams may be motivated by a desire for power, control, or a lack of leadership.

The Corporate Culture: This shark can create a toxic environment where employees feel undervalued, exploited, or powerless. Corporate cultures may be motivated by a desire for profit, efficiency, or a lack of ethical leadership.

Identifying these sharks is the first step to surviving in the corporate jungle. Once you know who they are and what they want, you can develop strategies to protect yourself and avoid becoming their prey.

THE PREDATORY MINDSET: HOW SHARKS THINK AND OPERATE

Understanding the predatory mindset is crucial for surviving in the corporate jungle. Sharks are not just ruthless individuals; they are also highly skilled predators with a specific set of strategies and tactics. By understanding how they think and operate, you can develop countermeasures to protect yourself and avoid becoming their prey.

The Desire for Power and Control: Sharks are often driven by a desire for power and control. They see the workplace as a hierarchy and strive to climb to the top. This can lead them to engage in manipulative and aggressive behaviors, such as bullying, intimidation, and sabotage.

The Focus on Self-Interest: Sharks are primarily concerned with their own interests. They may be willing to sacrifice the needs and goals of others to achieve their own ends. This can lead them to engage in unethical or illegal behavior, such as fraud, embezzlement, or discrimination.

The Ability to Manipulate Others: Sharks are often skilled manipulators. They may use flattery, deception, or intimidation to get what they want. They may also form alliances with others to strengthen their position and undermine their rivals.

The Fear of Failure: Sharks are often driven by a fear of failure. They may be willing to take risks or engage in unethical behavior to avoid being perceived as weak or incompetent. This can lead them to make impulsive decisions or act impulsively.

The Lack of Empathy: Sharks may have difficulty understanding or empathizing with the feelings of others. This can make them more likely to engage in harmful or exploitative behavior.

The Predatory Mindset: Sharks often adopt a predatory mindset. They view the workplace as a hunting ground and see their colleagues as potential prey. This can lead them to be constantly on the lookout for opportunities to exploit or undermine others.

The Survival Instinct: Sharks have a strong survival instinct. They are always looking for ways to protect themselves and advance their own interests. This can make them highly adaptable and resilient.

The Ability to Adapt: Sharks are able to adapt to changing circumstances. They are often quick to learn new skills or adopt new strategies. This can make them difficult to predict or outmaneuver.

The Focus on Results: Sharks are often results-oriented. They are more concerned with achieving their goals than with following rules or procedures. This can make them highly efficient, but it can also lead them to engage in unethical behavior.

The Ability to Network: Sharks are often skilled at networking. They are able to build relationships with influential people and leverage those connections to their advantage.

The Predatory Tactics: Sharks may use a variety of tactics to achieve their goals. These may include:
- **Bullying and intimidation:** Sharks may use threats or physical violence to intimidate others.
- **Manipulation:** Sharks may use flattery, deception, or guilt to get what they want.
- **Sabotage:** Sharks may try to ruin the plans or projects of others.
- **Backstabbing:** Sharks may spread rumors or undermine the reputation of others.
- **Gaslighting:** Sharks may try to make others doubt their own sanity.
- **Exploitation:** Sharks may take advantage of others for their own gain.
- **Corruption:** Sharks may engage in illegal or unethical behavior to achieve their goals.

Understanding the predatory mindset is essential for surviving in the corporate jungle. By recognizing the signs of predatory behavior and developing strategies to protect yourself, you can avoid becoming a victim and achieve your own goals.

Additional Tips for Dealing with Sharks:
- Build a strong network of allies.
- Document everything.
- Set boundaries.
- Be assertive.
- Don't be afraid to speak up.
- Seek help from a mentor or coach.
- Focus on your own goals.
- Develop a thick skin.
- Be resilient.
- Remember, you are not alone.

By following these tips, you can increase your chances of surviving in the corporate jungle and achieving your own goals.

CHAPTER 1
THE SHARK-INFESTED WATERS

THE CORPORATE JUNGLE: NAVIGATING THE TREACHEROUS WORKPLACE

The corporate world can be a treacherous place, filled with sharks and other predators. To survive and thrive in this environment, you need to understand the rules of the game and develop strategies to protect yourself and advance your career.

The Power Dynamics: The corporate world is a hierarchy, with power and influence concentrated at the top. Understanding the power dynamics is essential for navigating the workplace. Be aware of who the key players are, how they operate, and how you can leverage your position to your advantage.

The Office Politics: Office politics can be a major obstacle to career advancement. Be aware of the political landscape and avoid getting caught in the middle of power struggles. Build relationships with key players, but be careful not to become too dependent on any one person.

The Toxic Culture: Some companies have a toxic culture that can make it difficult to work there. If you find yourself in a toxic environment, try to find ways to improve the situation or consider leaving.

The Backstabbing and Betrayal: Backstabbing and betrayal are common in the corporate world. Be cautious about who you trust and avoid sharing sensitive information with anyone who might use it against you.

The Cutthroat Competition: Competition can be fierce in the corporate world. Be prepared to compete for promotions, raises, and other opportunities. However, avoid engaging in unethical or harmful behavior to get ahead.

The Glass Ceiling: The glass ceiling is a barrier that women and minorities often face in their careers. If you are a woman or a minority, be aware of the glass ceiling and be prepared to overcome it.

The Burnout: The demands of the corporate world can be stressful and can lead to burnout. Take care of yourself physically and mentally, and set boundaries between your work and personal life.

The Ethical Dilemmas: You may face ethical dilemmas in your career. Be prepared to make difficult decisions and stand up for what you believe in.

The Corporate Ladder: Climbing the corporate ladder can be a challenge. Be patient, persistent, and focused on your goals. Network with others, develop your skills, and take advantage of opportunities when they arise.

The Corporate Culture: Every company has its own unique culture. Understanding the culture can help you fit in and be successful.

The Diversity and Inclusion: Diversity and inclusion are becoming increasingly important in the corporate world. Embrace diversity and be an advocate for inclusion.

The Remote Work: The rise of remote work has changed the way we work. If you are a remote worker, be sure to stay connected with your team and maintain a strong work-life balance.

The Gig Economy: The gig economy is growing rapidly. If you are considering working in the gig economy, be prepared to be self-employed and manage your own finances.

The Future of Work: The future of work is uncertain. Be prepared to adapt to changes in the workplace, such as automation and artificial intelligence.

Tips for Navigating the Corporate Jungle:
- **Build a strong network of allies.**
- **Develop your skills and expertise.**
- **Be proactive and take initiative.**
- **Be resilient and persistent.**
- **Set boundaries and prioritize your well-being.**
- **Be ethical and honest in your dealings.**
- **Embrace diversity and inclusion.**
- **Stay informed about industry trends and developments.**
- **Be prepared to adapt to change.**
- **Remember, you are not alone.**

By following these tips, you can increase your chances of surviving and thriving in the corporate jungle.

THE SHARK-INFESTED MARKETPLACE: SURVIVING IN A COMPETITIVE WORLD

The modern professional operates in a cutthroat marketplace, where competition is fierce and the stakes are high. To survive and thrive in this shark-infested environment, you must develop a keen understanding of the competitive landscape and equip yourself with the necessary survival tactics.

The Competitive Landscape:
- **Global Competition:** The world economy is increasingly interconnected, meaning you're competing with professionals from around the globe. This presents both opportunities and challenges.
- **Rapid Technological Advancements:** Technology is disrupting industries at an unprecedented rate. Those who fail to adapt to these changes risk becoming obsolete.
- **Economic Uncertainty:** Economic fluctuations, such as recessions and market downturns, can create a challenging environment for businesses and professionals alike.
- **Changing Consumer Preferences:** Consumer tastes and behaviors are constantly evolving, making it imperative for businesses to stay ahead of the curve.
- **Increasing Regulation:** Government regulations can be burdensome for businesses, especially small and medium-sized enterprises.

Survival Tactics for the Modern Professional:
1. **Continuous Learning:** The pace of change in the modern workplace is rapid. To stay competitive, you must commit to lifelong learning. This includes acquiring new skills, staying up-to-date on industry trends, and seeking out opportunities for professional development.
2. **Adaptability and Resilience:** The ability to adapt to change is essential for survival in a competitive marketplace. Be prepared to embrace new technologies, work processes, and business models. Develop resilience to bounce back from setbacks and challenges.
3. **Strong Networking Skills:** Building and maintaining strong relationships is crucial for success in the modern business world. Network with

colleagues, clients, and industry experts to expand your professional circle and create opportunities.
4. **Effective Communication:** Clear and effective communication is essential for building relationships, closing deals, and resolving conflicts. Develop strong communication skills, both verbal and written.
5. **Problem-Solving and Critical Thinking:** The ability to solve complex problems and think critically is highly valued in today's job market. Develop your problem-solving skills and learn to analyze information objectively.
6. **Innovation and Creativity:** In a competitive marketplace, innovation is key. Look for ways to differentiate yourself and your business from the competition by developing new products, services, or business models.
7. **Ethical Conduct:** Maintaining a strong ethical code is essential for building trust and credibility. Avoid engaging in unethical or illegal practices, as they can have serious consequences.
8. **Work-Life Balance:** While it's important to be dedicated to your career, it's equally important to maintain a healthy work-life balance. Take care of your physical and mental health, and make time for activities you enjoy.
9. **Financial Literacy:** Understanding financial concepts, such as budgeting, investing, and debt management, is essential for achieving financial security.
10. **Personal Branding:** In today's digital age, personal branding is more important than ever. Create a strong online presence and cultivate a positive reputation.

Additional Tips for Surviving in a Competitive Marketplace:
- **Be proactive, not reactive.**

- **Take calculated risks.**
- **Be persistent and resilient.**
- **Don't be afraid to ask for help.**
- **Believe in yourself.**

By following these survival tactics, you can increase your chances of success in the competitive marketplace and avoid becoming a victim of the sharks. Remember, while the journey may be challenging, the rewards can be great.

CHAPTER 2
SHARK BAIT: COMMON MISTAKES

AVOID BECOMING PREY: UNDERSTANDING THE MISTAKES THAT MAKE YOU VULNERABLE

In the cutthroat world of business, mistakes can have serious consequences. Understanding the common pitfalls that can make you vulnerable to sharks is essential for survival. By avoiding these mistakes, you can protect yourself and increase your chances of success.

Overconfidence: While confidence is essential for success, overconfidence can be a major liability. Overestimating your abilities can lead to poor decision-making and make you more susceptible to manipulation.

Lack of Self-Awareness: A lack of self-awareness can make you vulnerable to exploitation. Understanding your strengths and weaknesses is essential for effective self-promotion and negotiation.

Fear of Failure: Fear of failure can paralyze you and prevent you from taking necessary risks. Overcoming this fear is crucial for career advancement.

Poor Time Management: Ineffective time management can lead to missed deadlines, decreased productivity, and a stressed-out work environment. Develop effective time management skills to avoid these pitfalls.

Lack of Networking: Building strong relationships is essential for success in the corporate world. Neglecting to network can limit your opportunities and make you more vulnerable to isolation.

Lack of Financial Literacy: A lack of financial knowledge can make you vulnerable to financial exploitation. Understanding basic financial concepts, such as budgeting, investing, and debt management, is essential for financial security.

Poor Communication Skills: Effective communication is essential for building relationships, resolving conflicts, and advancing your career. Poor communication skills can make you vulnerable to misunderstandings and misinterpretations.

Lack of Adaptability: The business world is constantly changing. A lack of adaptability can make you vulnerable to obsolescence. Stay up-to-date on industry trends and be willing to learn new skills.

Lack of Ethical Integrity: Compromising your ethical principles can damage your reputation and career. Always act with honesty and integrity.

Neglecting Your Mental and Physical Health: Neglecting your mental and physical health can lead to decreased productivity, increased stress, and a decline in overall well-being. Prioritize self-care to avoid these pitfalls.

Lack of Resilience: Resilience is the ability to bounce back from setbacks. A lack of resilience can make you vulnerable to giving up when faced with challenges.

Excessive Risk-Taking: Taking calculated risks is essential for success, but excessive risk-taking can lead to financial ruin and career setbacks.

Lack of Delegation: Trying to do everything yourself can lead to burnout and decreased productivity. Learn to delegate tasks effectively to free up your time and focus on high-priority activities.

Avoidance of Conflict: Conflict is a natural part of the workplace. Avoiding conflict can lead to resentment, decreased productivity, and damaged relationships. Learn to address conflicts constructively.

Overreliance on Others: Being overly dependent on others can make you vulnerable to manipulation and exploitation. Develop your own skills and abilities to become self-sufficient.

Lack of Professionalism: Unprofessional behavior can damage your reputation and career. Always conduct yourself with professionalism, even in challenging situations.

Neglecting Your Career Development: Neglecting your career development can limit your opportunities for advancement. Continuously seek out opportunities for professional growth and development.

Overlooking the Power of Mentorship: A mentor can provide valuable guidance and support. Seeking out a mentor can help you navigate the corporate world and avoid common pitfalls.

Failing to Set Boundaries: Setting boundaries is essential for maintaining a healthy work-life balance. Failing to set boundaries can lead to burnout and decreased productivity.

Overlooking the Importance of Diversity and Inclusion: Ignoring the importance of diversity and inclusion can create a hostile work environment and limit your opportunities. Embrace diversity and be an advocate for inclusion.

Avoiding Feedback: Seeking feedback is essential for growth and development. Avoiding feedback can prevent you from identifying and addressing your weaknesses.

Underestimating the Power of Networking: Building strong relationships is essential for success. Neglecting to network can limit your opportunities and make you more vulnerable to isolation.

Failing to Recognize the Importance of Personal Branding: In today's digital age, personal branding is more important than ever. Neglecting your personal brand can limit your visibility and opportunities.

By avoiding these common mistakes, you can increase your chances of success in the corporate world and avoid becoming a victim of the sharks. Remember, while the journey may be challenging, the rewards can be great.

PART II

Developing Shark Survival Skills

CHAPTER 3
THE ARMOR OF CONFIDENCE

BUILDING SELF-ESTEEM: BELIEVING IN YOUR ABILITIES

Self-esteem is the foundation of success in the corporate world. It's the belief in yourself, your abilities, and your worth. When you have high self-esteem, you're more confident, resilient, and capable of achieving your goals.

Understanding Self-Esteem:
Self-esteem is not about arrogance or ego. It's about having a healthy sense of self-worth and believing in your ability to overcome challenges. When you have high self-esteem, you're more likely to take risks, persevere through setbacks, and achieve your goals.

Factors Affecting Self-Esteem:
Several factors can influence your self-esteem, including:
- **Childhood experiences:** Negative experiences in childhood, such as bullying, abuse, or rejection, can have a lasting impact on self-esteem.
- **Social comparisons:** Comparing yourself to others can lead to feelings of inadequacy and low self-esteem.
- **Negative self-talk:** Negative thoughts and self-criticism can erode self-esteem.
- **Lack of achievement:** A lack of success or accomplishment can contribute to low self-esteem.

Building Self-Esteem:
Building self-esteem takes time and effort, but it's a worthwhile investment. Here are some strategies to help you boost your self-esteem:

How To Swim With The Sharks Without Being Eaten Alive

- **Challenge negative thoughts:** Identify and challenge negative thoughts about yourself. Replace them with positive affirmations.
- **Focus on your strengths:** Acknowledge and celebrate your strengths and accomplishments.
- **Set realistic goals:** Set achievable goals and celebrate your successes.
- **Practice self-care:** Take care of your physical and mental health.
- **Surround yourself with positive people:** Spend time with people who support and encourage you.
- **Learn to accept compliments:** Don't dismiss compliments as flattery. Accept them graciously.
- **Practice self-compassion:** Be kind and forgiving to yourself.
- **Seek professional help:** If you're struggling with low self-esteem, consider seeking help from a therapist or counselor.

The Benefits of High Self-Esteem:
High self-esteem has numerous benefits, including:
- **Increased confidence:** When you believe in yourself, you're more confident and assertive.
- **Improved relationships:** High self-esteem can help you build stronger relationships with others.
- **Enhanced resilience:** People with high self-esteem are better able to bounce back from setbacks.
- **Greater success:** High self-esteem is associated with greater success in both personal and professional life.

Overcoming Self-Doubt:
Self-doubt is a common experience. However, it's important to recognize that self-doubt is often irrational and can be overcome. Here are some strategies for overcoming self-doubt:

- **Challenge negative thoughts:** Identify and challenge negative thoughts about your abilities.
- **Focus on your strengths:** Remind yourself of your accomplishments and positive qualities.
- **Seek support:** Talk to friends, family, or a mentor for encouragement and support.
- **Take small steps:** Break down large goals into smaller, more manageable steps.
- **Celebrate your successes:** No matter how small, celebrate your achievements.

Building self-esteem is an ongoing process. It requires patience, persistence, and a commitment to self-improvement. By following these strategies, you can develop a strong sense of self-worth and achieve your goals.

PROJECTING CONFIDENCE: COMMUNICATING ASSERTIVELY

In the competitive world of business, projecting confidence is essential for success. It allows you to command respect, influence others, and negotiate effectively. However, confidence is not about arrogance or aggression. It's about communicating assertively, expressing your needs and opinions clearly and respectfully.

Understanding Assertiveness:

Assertiveness is the ability to express your thoughts, feelings, and needs in a direct, honest, and respectful manner. It's about standing up for yourself without being aggressive or passive. Assertive communication involves:
- **Clear and direct communication:** Expressing your thoughts and feelings clearly and concisely.
- **Respectful communication:** Communicating in a way that respects the feelings and opinions of others.

- **Appropriate nonverbal communication:** Using body language, tone of voice, and facial expressions that convey confidence and assertiveness.

The Benefits of Assertive Communication:

Assertive communication has numerous benefits, including:
- **Improved relationships:** Assertive communication can help you build stronger relationships with others.
- **Increased self-esteem:** Expressing yourself assertively can boost your self-confidence and self-esteem.
- **Enhanced career success:** Assertive communication is essential for career advancement and success.
- **Reduced stress:** Assertive communication can help you manage stress and avoid conflict.

Overcoming Passivity and Aggressiveness:

Many people struggle with either passive or aggressive communication styles. Passivity involves avoiding expressing your needs or opinions, while aggressiveness involves expressing them in a hostile or domineering manner. Both styles can be harmful to your relationships and career.

To overcome passivity, it's important to learn to express your needs and opinions clearly and respectfully. Practice saying "no" when necessary, and don't be afraid to ask for what you want.

To overcome aggressiveness, it's important to learn to control your emotions and communicate calmly and respectfully. Avoid using insults, threats, or other forms of verbal abuse.

Strategies for Assertive Communication:
- **Use "I" statements:** "I" statements help you express your feelings and needs without blaming others. For

example, instead of saying "You're always late," say "I feel frustrated when you're late."
- **Practice active listening:** Pay attention to what the other person is saying and show that you're listening.
- **Use nonverbal cues:** Use body language, tone of voice, and facial expressions that convey confidence and assertiveness.
- **Set boundaries:** Learn to set boundaries and stick to them.
- **Practice assertiveness:** Practice assertive communication in low-stakes situations until you feel comfortable.
- **Seek professional help:** If you're struggling with assertiveness, consider seeking help from a therapist or counselor.

Building Confidence:

Confidence is essential for assertive communication. Here are some strategies for building confidence:

- **Challenge negative thoughts:** Identify and challenge negative thoughts about yourself.
- **Focus on your strengths:** Acknowledge and celebrate your strengths and accomplishments.
- **Set realistic goals:** Set achievable goals and celebrate your successes.
- **Practice self-care:** Take care of your physical and mental health.
- **Surround yourself with positive people:** Spend time with people who support and encourage you.
- **Seek feedback:** Ask for feedback from trusted friends, colleagues, or mentors.
- **Take risks:** Step outside of your comfort zone and take calculated risks.

Additional Tips for Assertive Communication:

- **Be prepared:** Prepare what you want to say before a difficult conversation.
- **Choose the right time and place:** Choose a time and place where you can have an uninterrupted conversation.
- **Stay calm and collected:** Avoid getting emotional or defensive.
- **Be willing to compromise:** Be open to finding a solution that works for everyone.
- **Don't give up:** If you don't get the desired outcome, don't give up. Keep practicing assertive communication.

By mastering the art of assertive communication, you can improve your relationships, enhance your career, and achieve your goals. Remember, confidence is not about being perfect. It's about believing in yourself and your ability to communicate effectively.

CHAPTER 4
THE ART OF DECEPTION

STRATEGIC BLUFFING: USING DECEPTION TO YOUR ADVANTAGE

Bluffing is often associated with dishonesty and manipulation. However, when used strategically and ethically, bluffing can be a powerful tool for negotiation, persuasion, and self-defense. In the competitive world of business, knowing how to bluff effectively can give you a significant advantage.

Understanding Bluffing:
Bluffing is a form of deception that involves deliberately misrepresenting information to achieve a desired outcome. It's not about lying outright, but rather about creating a perception of reality that benefits you. When used strategically, bluffing can be a powerful tool for negotiation, persuasion, and self-defense.

Ethical Considerations:
While bluffing can be a useful tactic, it's important to use it ethically. Avoid lying about facts or making false promises. Instead, focus on creating a perception of reality that is consistent with your goals.

When to Bluff:
Bluffing is most effective when used in situations where the stakes are high and the potential rewards outweigh the risks. Some common scenarios where bluffing may be useful include:
- **Negotiations:** Bluffing can be a powerful tool for negotiating better deals. By creating a perception of

scarcity or urgency, you can increase your bargaining power.
- **Persuasion:** Bluffing can be used to persuade others to agree to your point of view. By exaggerating the benefits of your proposal or the consequences of rejection, you can increase your chances of success.
- **Self-defense:** Bluffing can be used to protect yourself from exploitation or harm. By creating a perception of strength or danger, you can deter potential threats.

Bluffing Strategies:
- **Create a perception of scarcity:** Make it appear as though your offer or opportunity is limited or in high demand.
- **Exaggerate your options:** Make it seem like you have many other options available to you.
- **Downplay your needs:** Make it appear as though you don't need a particular deal or outcome.
- **Use silence as a weapon:** Silence can be a powerful tool for creating uncertainty and doubt.
- **Be prepared to back down:** If your bluff is called, be prepared to back down gracefully.

Reading Others:
To use bluffing effectively, you need to be able to read others. Pay attention to their body language, facial expressions, and tone of voice. Look for signs of doubt, uncertainty, or fear.

Building Credibility:
Bluffing is more effective when you have a strong reputation for honesty and integrity. Avoid lying or making false promises, as this will erode your credibility.

Ethical Considerations:
While bluffing can be a useful tactic, it's important to use it ethically. Avoid lying about facts or making false promises. Instead, focus on creating a perception of reality that is consistent with your goals.

The Dangers of Bluffing:
Bluffing can be risky. If your bluff is called, it can damage your reputation and credibility. It's important to weigh the potential benefits and risks before deciding to bluff.

Alternative Strategies:
If you're uncomfortable with bluffing, there are other strategies you can use to achieve your goals. These include:
- **Building relationships:** Building strong relationships with others can give you an advantage in negotiations and persuasion.
- **Providing value:** Offering value to others can make them more likely to cooperate with you.
- **Being persuasive:** Developing strong persuasion skills can help you convince others to agree to your point of view.
- **Negotiating effectively:** Learning effective negotiation techniques can help you get the best possible deals.

Bluffing can be a powerful tool for achieving your goals, but it must be used strategically and ethically. By understanding the principles of bluffing and using it wisely, you can increase your chances of success in the competitive world of business.

ADVANCED NEGOTIATION TACTICS

In the competitive world of business, negotiation is an essential skill. Effective negotiation can help you secure better deals, resolve conflicts, and achieve your goals. However, negotiation is not just about haggling over price. It's about understanding your interests, the interests of the other party, and finding mutually beneficial solutions.

Understanding Negotiation:
Negotiation is a process of bargaining to reach a mutually acceptable agreement. It involves a combination of strategy, tactics, and interpersonal skills. Effective negotiation requires a deep understanding of your own goals, the goals of the other party, and the underlying interests of both parties.

Key Negotiation Strategies:
- **BATNA:** Your Best Alternative to a Negotiated Agreement (BATNA) is your fallback option. Knowing your BATNA gives you leverage in negotiations.
- **Reservation Price:** Your reservation price is the minimum acceptable outcome for you.
- **Zone of Possible Agreement (ZOPA):** The ZOPA is the range of outcomes that are acceptable to both parties.
- **Anchoring:** Anchoring is a technique used to influence the other party's perception of a fair outcome.
- **Framing:** Framing refers to the way information is presented. By framing information in a way that benefits you, you can influence the outcome of negotiations.
- **Leverage:** Leverage is the power you have to influence the outcome of negotiations. It can be based on your BATNA, your expertise, or your relationships.
- **Trade-offs:** Trade-offs are concessions that you make in exchange for something else.
- **BATNA:** Your Best Alternative to a Negotiated Agreement (BATNA) is your fallback option. Knowing your BATNA gives you leverage in negotiations.
- **Reservation Price:** Your reservation price is the minimum acceptable outcome for you.

- **Zone of Possible Agreement (ZOPA):** The ZOPA is the range of outcomes that are acceptable to both parties.
- **Anchoring:** Anchoring is a technique used to influence the other party's perception of a fair outcome.
- **Framing:** Framing refers to the way information is presented. By framing information in a way that benefits you, you can influence the outcome of negotiations.
- **Leverage:** Leverage is the power you have to influence the outcome of negotiations. It can be based on your BATNA, your expertise, or your relationships.
- **Trade-offs:** Trade-offs are concessions that you make in exchange for something else.

Advanced Negotiation Tactics:
- **Distributive Negotiation:** Distributive negotiation is a win-lose strategy where one party gains at the expense of the other.
- **Integrative Negotiation:** Integrative negotiation is a win-win strategy where both parties benefit from the agreement.
- **Interest-Based Negotiation:** Interest-based negotiation focuses on underlying interests rather than positions.
- **Power Plays:** Power plays are tactics used to gain an advantage in negotiations.
- **Bluffing:** Bluffing is a risky strategy that involves exaggerating your position or making false claims.
- **Time Pressure:** Using time pressure can be a powerful negotiation tactic.

Preparing for Negotiations:
- **Do your research:** Gather as much information as possible about the other party and the issues being negotiated.

- **Set goals:** Clearly define your goals and priorities.
- **Develop a strategy:** Develop a negotiation strategy based on your goals and the information you have gathered.
- **Practice:** Practice your negotiation skills with a friend or colleague.

Negotiation Techniques:
- **Active listening:** Pay attention to what the other party is saying and ask clarifying questions.
- **Empathy:** Try to understand the other party's perspective.
- **Be patient:** Negotiations can be time-consuming. Be patient and persistent.
- **Be flexible:** Be willing to compromise and find mutually beneficial solutions.
- **Avoid ultimatums:** Ultimatums can be counterproductive.
- **Close the deal:** Once you've reached an agreement, be sure to close the deal.

Post-Negotiation Analysis:

After a negotiation, it's important to reflect on the process and identify areas for improvement. This can help you become a more effective negotiator in the future.

Ethical Considerations:

It's important to negotiate ethically. Avoid using manipulative or deceptive tactics. Always treat the other party with respect.

Negotiation is a valuable skill that can help you achieve your goals and succeed in the corporate world. By understanding the key strategies and techniques, you can become a more effective negotiator and improve your chances of success.

THE POWER OF PERSUASION

In the competitive world of business, the ability to persuade others is a valuable asset. Whether you're trying to sell a product, negotiate a deal, or motivate a team, persuasion is essential for success.

Understanding Persuasion:
Persuasion is the art of influencing others to believe or do something. It's not about manipulation or trickery. It's about presenting your ideas in a way that is compelling, persuasive, and convincing.

Key Elements of Persuasion:
- **Credibility:** People are more likely to be persuaded by someone who is credible and trustworthy.
- **Trust:** Building trust is essential for persuasion. People are more likely to be persuaded by someone they trust.
- **Likability:** People are more likely to be persuaded by someone they like and respect.
- **Expertise:** People are more likely to be persuaded by someone who is knowledgeable and experienced.
- **Social proof:** People are more likely to be persuaded by the opinions of others.
- **Scarcity:** People are more likely to be persuaded by something that is scarce or limited.
- **Authority:** People are more likely to be persuaded by someone who is perceived as an authority figure.

Persuasive Techniques:
- **Storytelling:** Stories can be a powerful tool for persuasion. By telling stories, you can connect with your audience on an emotional level.

- **Rhetorical devices:** Rhetorical devices, such as metaphors, similes, and analogies, can make your arguments more persuasive.
- **Emotional appeals:** Appealing to people's emotions can be a powerful persuasive technique.
- **Logical arguments:** Presenting logical arguments can be persuasive, especially when dealing with rational people.
- **Call to action:** A clear call to action can encourage people to take the desired action.

Overcoming Objections:
When presenting your ideas, be prepared to address objections. Here are some strategies for overcoming objections:
- **Anticipate objections:** Anticipate potential objections and prepare your responses in advance.
- **Acknowledge objections:** Acknowledge the other person's point of view, even if you disagree.
- **Address concerns:** Address the other person's concerns and provide solutions.
- **Be prepared to compromise:** Be willing to compromise to reach an agreement.

Building Credibility:
Building credibility is essential for persuasion. Here are some tips for building credibility:
- **Demonstrate expertise:** Show that you are knowledgeable and experienced in your field.
- **Be authentic:** Be yourself and avoid trying to be someone you're not.
- **Build relationships:** Build strong relationships with others.
- **Be ethical:** Be honest and trustworthy.

The Power of Persuasion:
Persuasion is a valuable skill that can help you achieve your goals. By understanding the key elements of persuasion and using effective techniques, you can influence others to believe and do what you want.

Additional Tips for Persuasion:
- **Practice active listening:** Pay attention to what the other person is saying and ask clarifying questions.
- **Use body language effectively:** Use body language to convey confidence and credibility.
- **Be patient:** Persuasion takes time. Be patient and persistent.
- **Be flexible:** Be willing to adapt your approach based on the situation.
- **Celebrate your successes:** Celebrate your successes and use them to build your credibility.

By mastering the art of persuasion, you can become a more effective leader, negotiator, and communicator.

READING OTHERS: UNDERSTANDING THEIR INTENTIONS

In the corporate jungle, understanding the intentions of others is crucial for survival. By being able to read people and decipher their motives, you can avoid being manipulated, exploited, or betrayed.

The Importance of Reading Others:
Understanding the intentions of others is essential for:
- **Building relationships:** People are more likely to trust and cooperate with those they perceive as honest and trustworthy.

- **Avoiding conflict:** By understanding the motivations of others, you can avoid misunderstandings and conflicts.
- **Negotiating effectively:** Knowing the needs and wants of others can help you negotiate better deals.
- **Protecting yourself:** Being able to read people can help you identify potential threats and avoid being manipulated or exploited.

Nonverbal Communication:

Nonverbal communication is a powerful tool for understanding the intentions of others. Pay attention to their body language, facial expressions, and tone of voice. These cues can provide valuable insights into their thoughts and feelings.

- **Body language:** Look for signs of nervousness, such as fidgeting or avoiding eye contact. Pay attention to posture, gestures, and overall body language.
- **Facial expressions:** Facial expressions can reveal emotions such as happiness, sadness, anger, and fear.
- **Tone of voice:** Listen to the tone of voice. A person's voice can reveal a lot about their emotions and intentions.

Verbal Cues:

Verbal cues can also provide valuable insights into the intentions of others. Pay attention to the words they use, the way they speak, and the topics they choose to discuss.

- **Word choice:** The words people use can reveal a lot about their thoughts and feelings. For example, people who use negative language may be feeling angry or resentful.
- **Speaking style:** Pay attention to the way people speak. Are they hesitant, evasive, or overly confident?
- **Topics of conversation:** The topics people choose to discuss can reveal their interests and priorities.

Patterns of Behavior:

Observing patterns of behavior can also help you understand the intentions of others. Look for consistent behaviors that may indicate a particular motive or personality trait.

- **Consistency:** Do people's actions align with their words? Are they consistent in their behavior?
- **Patterns of behavior:** Are there any recurring patterns in their behavior? For example, do they always try to dominate conversations or avoid taking responsibility?

Common Motivations:

Understanding common human motivations can also help you interpret the intentions of others. Some common motivations include:

- **Power:** People may be motivated by a desire for power or control.
- **Status:** People may be motivated by a desire for status or recognition.
- **Money:** People may be motivated by a desire for financial gain.
- **Fear:** People may be motivated by fear of failure, rejection, or loss.
- **Love:** People may be motivated by a desire for love, affection, or belonging.

The Dangers of Assumptions:

While reading others can be a valuable skill, it's important to avoid making assumptions. Assumptions can lead to misunderstandings and conflicts. Always seek to verify your observations and assumptions before making judgments.

How To Swim With The Sharks Without Being Eaten Alive

Developing Your People-Reading Skills:

Developing your people-reading skills takes time and practice. Here are some tips for improving your ability to understand the intentions of others:

- **Observe people closely:** Pay attention to their body language, facial expressions, and verbal cues.
- **Ask questions:** Ask open-ended questions to get people to talk about themselves and their motivations.
- **Seek feedback:** Ask trusted friends or colleagues for feedback on your people-reading skills.
- **Practice empathy:** Try to understand the perspective of others.
- **Be mindful of your own biases:** Be aware of your own biases and how they may affect your perceptions.

By developing your people-reading skills, you can improve your relationships, avoid conflicts, and protect yourself from manipulation. Remember, understanding the intentions of others is not about mind-reading. It's about being observant, empathetic, and using your intuition.

CHAPTER 5
THE POWER OF NETWORKING

BUILDING ALLIANCES: FORMING RELATIONSHIPS WITH INFLUENTIAL PEOPLE

In the corporate jungle, building strong relationships with influential people can be a powerful tool for survival and success. By forming alliances with key players, you can gain access to opportunities, resources, and support that would otherwise be unavailable.

The Importance of Alliances:
Building alliances can provide numerous benefits, including:
- **Increased visibility:** Being associated with influential people can increase your visibility and credibility.
- **Access to opportunities:** Influential people can open doors to new opportunities and projects.
- **Support and mentorship:** Mentors can provide guidance, support, and advice.
- **Protection:** Having strong relationships with influential people can protect you from political attacks or sabotage.
- **Increased bargaining power:** Alliances can give you greater bargaining power in negotiations.

Identifying Influential People:
Influential people come in all shapes and sizes. They may be senior executives, industry leaders, thought leaders, or simply people with a large network of contacts. Here are some ways to identify influential people:

- **Look for leadership roles:** People in leadership positions, such as CEOs, presidents, or department heads, are often influential.
- **Identify industry experts:** People who are recognized as experts in their field are often influential.
- **Look for people with large networks:** People with large networks of contacts can be valuable allies.
- **Pay attention to who people listen to:** If people often seek out the advice or opinion of a particular individual, they are likely influential.

Building Relationships:

Once you've identified some influential people, the next step is to build relationships with them. Here are some tips for building strong alliances:

- **Network strategically:** Attend industry events, conferences, and networking functions.
- **Offer value:** Don't just ask for favors. Offer value to others by sharing your knowledge, expertise, or connections.
- **Be authentic:** Be yourself and build relationships based on mutual respect and trust.
- **Follow up:** After meeting someone new, follow up with a thank-you note or email.
- **Be patient:** Building strong relationships takes time and effort. Don't expect instant results.

Maintaining Relationships:

Once you've formed an alliance, it's important to maintain the relationship. Here are some tips for maintaining strong alliances:

- **Keep in touch:** Stay in touch with your allies on a regular basis.
- **Offer support:** Be there for your allies when they need you.
- **Be reliable:** Be a reliable and trustworthy ally.

- **Avoid conflicts of interest:** Avoid situations that could compromise your relationship.

Leveraging Your Alliances:

Once you've built strong alliances, you can leverage them to achieve your goals. Here are some ways to leverage your alliances:

- **Seek advice and guidance:** Ask your allies for advice and guidance on career matters.
- **Request referrals:** Ask your allies for referrals to potential clients, employers, or business partners.
- **Collaborate on projects:** Collaborate with your allies on projects that can benefit both of you.
- **Negotiate better deals:** Use your alliances to negotiate better deals and terms.
- **Protect yourself from political attacks:** Having strong alliances can protect you from political attacks or sabotage.

The Dangers of Overreliance:

While alliances can be a powerful tool, it's important to avoid becoming overly reliant on any one person. Overreliance can make you vulnerable to manipulation or exploitation.

Building Your Own Network:

In addition to building alliances with influential people, it's also important to build your own network of contacts. This will give you greater independence and flexibility.

Building alliances is a valuable skill that can help you achieve your goals in the corporate world. By identifying influential people, building relationships, and leveraging your alliances, you can increase your visibility, access to opportunities, and overall success.

LEVERAGING YOUR NETWORK: USING CONNECTIONS TO YOUR ADVANTAGE

In the competitive world of business, your network is one of your most valuable assets. By leveraging your connections effectively, you can open doors to new opportunities, gain access to valuable resources, and build a strong reputation.

The Power of Your Network:
Your network is the people you know, both personally and professionally. It includes your colleagues, clients, mentors, friends, and family. When used strategically, your network can provide you with:
- **Information and insights:** Your network can provide you with valuable information and insights into your industry, the job market, and potential opportunities.
- **Opportunities:** Your network can connect you with potential clients, employers, and business partners.
- **Support and mentorship:** Your network can provide you with support, guidance, and mentorship.
- **Protection:** Your network can protect you from political attacks or sabotage.
- **Increased bargaining power:** Your network can give you greater bargaining power in negotiations.

Building Your Network:
To leverage your network effectively, you need to build strong relationships with people. Here are some tips for building your network:
- **Attend industry events:** Attend conferences, trade shows, and networking events to meet new people.

- **Join professional organizations:** Joining professional organizations can connect you with people in your industry.
- **Volunteer:** Volunteering can help you meet people with similar interests and values.
- **Use social media:** Social media can be a powerful tool for networking.
- **Be proactive:** Don't just wait for people to reach out to you. Be proactive and initiate contact.

Maintaining Your Network:

Once you've built your network, it's important to maintain it. Here are some tips for maintaining your relationships:

- **Stay in touch:** Keep in touch with your contacts on a regular basis.
- **Offer value:** Don't just ask for favors. Offer value to others by sharing your knowledge, expertise, or connections.
- **Be reliable:** Be a reliable and trustworthy ally.
- **Avoid conflicts of interest:** Avoid situations that could compromise your relationships.

Leveraging Your Network:

Once you've built a strong network, you can leverage it to achieve your goals. Here are some ways to use your network to your advantage:

- **Seek advice and guidance:** Ask your network for advice and guidance on career matters.
- **Request referrals:** Ask your network for referrals to potential clients, employers, or business partners.
- **Collaborate on projects:** Collaborate with your network on projects that can benefit both of you.
- **Negotiate better deals:** Use your network to negotiate better deals and terms.

- **Protect yourself from political attacks:** Having a strong network can protect you from political attacks or sabotage.

The Dangers of Overreliance:
While your network can be a valuable asset, it's important to avoid becoming overly reliant on any one person or group. Overreliance can make you vulnerable to manipulation or exploitation.

Building Your Own Network:
In addition to leveraging your existing network, it's also important to build your own network. This will give you greater independence and flexibility.

Your network is one of your most valuable assets in the corporate world. By building strong relationships and leveraging your connections effectively, you can increase your visibility, access to opportunities, and overall success.

PART III

Outmaneuvering the Sharks

CHAPTER 6
THE PREDATOR BECOMES THE PREY

TURNING THE TABLES: TAKING CONTROL OF THE SITUATION

In the corporate jungle, it's often necessary to take control of the situation to avoid becoming prey. By understanding the dynamics of power and manipulation, you can turn the tables and gain the upper hand.

Understanding Power Dynamics:
The corporate world is a hierarchy, with power and influence concentrated at the top. Understanding the power dynamics is essential for navigating the workplace and taking control of situations.
- **Identify key players:** Identify the most influential people in your organization.
- **Understand their motivations:** Understand what motivates these individuals.
- **Leverage your position:** Use your position and relationships to gain leverage.

Recognizing Manipulation:
Manipulation is a common tactic used by sharks to control others. Be aware of the signs of manipulation, such as:
- **Gaslighting:** Making you doubt your own reality.
- **Triangulation:** Playing you against others.
- **Guilt-tripping:** Making you feel guilty for not doing what they want.
- **Emotional blackmail:** Threatening to harm themselves or others if you don't do what they want.

Defending Against Manipulation:

If you're being manipulated, it's important to defend yourself. Here are some strategies for defending against manipulation:

- **Call them out:** Confront the manipulator and let them know that their behavior is unacceptable.
- **Set boundaries:** Establish clear boundaries and stick to them.
- **Document everything:** Keep a record of the manipulator's behavior.
- **Seek support:** Talk to a trusted friend, colleague, or mentor for support.

Taking Control of the Situation:

Once you've identified the power dynamics and recognized manipulation tactics, you can begin to take control of the situation. Here are some strategies for turning the tables:

- **Build a strong network:** Build relationships with influential people who can support you.
- **Develop your skills and expertise:** The more skilled and knowledgeable you are, the more power you will have.
- **Be assertive:** Express your needs and opinions clearly and confidently.
- **Set boundaries:** Establish clear boundaries and stick to them.
- **Negotiate effectively:** Learn effective negotiation techniques to get what you want.
- **Be proactive:** Take initiative and don't wait for opportunities to come to you.
- **Build your reputation:** Build a positive reputation for yourself as a trustworthy and reliable professional.

Turning the Tables on a Toxic Boss:

If you're working for a toxic boss, it can be difficult to take control of the situation. However, there are steps you can take to improve the situation or find a new job.

- **Document everything:** Keep a record of your boss's abusive behavior.
- **Seek support:** Talk to a trusted friend, colleague, or mentor for support.
- **Consider legal action:** If your boss is breaking the law, you may have legal recourse.
- **Start job hunting:** If the situation is unbearable, start looking for a new job.

Turning the Tables on a Toxic Coworker:

If you're working with a toxic coworker, it can be difficult to maintain a positive work environment. Here are some strategies for dealing with toxic coworkers:

- **Set boundaries:** Establish clear boundaries and stick to them.
- **Avoid engaging in drama:** Don't get caught up in the toxic coworker's drama.
- **Document everything:** Keep a record of the toxic coworker's behavior.
- **Report the behavior:** If the behavior is severe, report it to your supervisor or HR department.

Turning the Tables on a Toxic Company Culture:

If you're working in a toxic company culture, it can be difficult to thrive. Here are some strategies for improving the situation:

- **Speak up:** Talk to your supervisor or HR department about your concerns.
- **Build a support network:** Connect with other employees who are unhappy with the company culture.
- **Consider leaving:** If the situation is unbearable, start looking for a new job.

Turning the tables in the corporate jungle requires courage, resilience, and a willingness to take action. By understanding the power dynamics, recognizing manipulation, and taking control of the situation, you can avoid becoming prey and achieve your goals.

SETTING BOUNDARIES: PROTECTING YOURSELF FROM EXPLOITATION

In the cutthroat world of business, setting boundaries is essential for protecting yourself from exploitation. Boundaries are limits that you establish to protect your physical, emotional, and mental well-being. By setting clear boundaries, you can avoid being taken advantage of, maintain a healthy work-life balance, and achieve your goals.

Understanding Boundaries:
Boundaries are limits that you set for yourself. They can be physical, emotional, or mental. For example, you might set a boundary about the number of hours you work, the amount of time you spend on projects, or the way you are treated by others.

The Importance of Boundaries:
Setting boundaries is essential for:
- **Protecting yourself from exploitation:** When you set boundaries, you are less likely to be taken advantage of by others.
- **Maintaining a healthy work-life balance:** Boundaries can help you avoid burnout and maintain a healthy work-life balance.
- **Building self-respect:** When you set and maintain boundaries, you are showing yourself that you respect your own needs and limits.

- **Improving relationships:** Clear boundaries can help you build stronger relationships with others.

Setting Effective Boundaries:
Setting effective boundaries requires clear communication, assertiveness, and consistency. Here are some tips for setting boundaries:
- **Be clear and direct:** When communicating your boundaries, be clear and direct. Avoid being vague or passive-aggressive.
- **Be assertive:** Express your boundaries assertively, without being aggressive or passive.
- **Be consistent:** Stick to your boundaries, even when it's difficult.
- **Be prepared for resistance:** Some people may resist your boundaries. Be prepared to respond calmly and assertively.
- **Practice self-care:** Take care of yourself physically and mentally. This will help you maintain your boundaries and avoid feeling overwhelmed.

Common Boundary Issues:
Some common boundary issues include:
- **Overworking:** Setting boundaries around your work hours can help you avoid burnout.
- **Saying no:** It's important to learn to say no when you're feeling overwhelmed or overextended.
- **Dealing with difficult people:** Setting boundaries can help you deal with difficult people in a healthy way.
- **Managing your time effectively:** Setting boundaries around your time can help you manage your workload more effectively.

Overcoming Challenges:
Setting and maintaining boundaries can be challenging. Here are some tips for overcoming challenges:

- **Start small:** Start by setting small, manageable boundaries.
- **Practice assertiveness:** Practice expressing your boundaries assertively.
- **Seek support:** Talk to a friend, family member, or therapist for support.
- **Be patient:** Building boundaries takes time and practice.

The Benefits of Setting Boundaries:

Setting boundaries can have numerous benefits, including:

- **Increased self-esteem:** When you set boundaries, you are showing yourself that you respect your own needs and limits.
- **Improved relationships:** Clear boundaries can help you build stronger relationships with others.
- **Reduced stress:** Setting boundaries can help you reduce stress and avoid burnout.
- **Increased productivity:** When you set boundaries, you are more likely to be productive and focused.

Setting boundaries is an essential skill for surviving in the corporate jungle. By protecting yourself from exploitation and maintaining a healthy work-life balance, you can achieve your goals and live a more fulfilling life.

CHAPTER 7
THE ART OF SURVIVAL

ADAPTING TO CHANGE: EMBRACING UNCERTAINTY

In today's rapidly evolving business landscape, the ability to adapt to change is crucial for survival. The modern professional must be prepared to embrace uncertainty and navigate a constantly changing environment.

The Importance of Adaptability:
Adaptability is the ability to adjust to new situations and challenges. It's a vital skill for success in the modern workplace, where change is the only constant. Adaptable professionals are more resilient, innovative, and able to seize opportunities.

Understanding Uncertainty:
Uncertainty is the state of not knowing what will happen. It can be caused by factors such as economic fluctuations, technological advancements, industry disruptions, and global events. Embracing uncertainty means accepting that the future is unpredictable and being prepared to adapt to changing circumstances.

Overcoming Fear of Change:
Fear of change is a common human emotion. However, it can hinder your ability to adapt and thrive in a rapidly changing environment. To overcome fear of change, it's important to:
- **Challenge negative thoughts:** Identify and challenge negative thoughts about change.
- **Focus on the positive:** Look for the opportunities and benefits that change can bring.

- **Step outside your comfort zone:** Embrace new challenges and experiences.
- **Seek support:** Talk to friends, family, or a mentor for support.

Strategies for Adapting to Change:
- **Stay informed:** Stay up-to-date on industry trends and developments.
- **Develop a growth mindset:** Believe that you can learn and grow, even in challenging situations.
- **Be flexible:** Be willing to adjust your plans and expectations as needed.
- **Embrace continuous learning:** Commit to lifelong learning and skill development.
- **Build a strong network:** A strong network can provide you with support, information, and opportunities.
- **Practice mindfulness:** Mindfulness can help you stay calm and focused in the face of uncertainty.
- **Develop resilience:** Build your resilience by learning to cope with setbacks and challenges.

Leveraging Change as an Opportunity:

Rather than fearing change, you can leverage it as an opportunity for growth and innovation. Here are some strategies for turning change into a positive:
- **Identify trends:** Stay ahead of the curve by identifying emerging trends in your industry.
- **Innovate:** Develop new products, services, or business models to meet changing customer needs.
- **Collaborate:** Partner with others to develop innovative solutions.
- **Take calculated risks:** Be willing to take calculated risks to seize new opportunities.
- **Embrace failure:** View failure as a learning opportunity, rather than a setback.

Embracing Uncertainty:
Embracing uncertainty means accepting that the future is unpredictable and being prepared to adapt to changing circumstances. It's about developing a mindset of resilience, adaptability, and innovation. By embracing uncertainty, you can position yourself for success in today's rapidly changing world.

Additional Tips for Adapting to Change:
- **Develop a positive attitude:** A positive attitude can help you overcome challenges and find opportunities.
- **Be patient:** Change takes time. Be patient and persistent.
- **Seek feedback:** Ask for feedback from others to identify areas for improvement.
- **Celebrate your successes:** Celebrate your achievements, no matter how small.
- **Remember, you are not alone:** Many people are facing similar challenges. Seek support from others.

By embracing uncertainty and developing the skills necessary to adapt to change, you can thrive in today's rapidly evolving business landscape.

MAINTAINING RESILIENCE: BOUNCING BACK FROM SETBACKS

In the competitive world of business, setbacks are inevitable. The ability to bounce back from adversity, known as resilience, is a crucial skill for survival and success. Resilient individuals are better equipped to handle challenges, overcome obstacles, and achieve their goals.

Understanding Resilience:
Resilience is the ability to adapt to change, overcome adversity, and bounce back from setbacks. It's a combination

of mental, emotional, and behavioral traits that allow individuals to cope with challenges and thrive.

Factors Affecting Resilience:
Several factors can influence your resilience, including:
- **Childhood experiences:** Positive childhood experiences can foster resilience.
- **Social support:** Strong social connections can provide emotional support and encouragement.
- **Optimism:** A positive outlook can help you see challenges as opportunities for growth.
- **Self-esteem:** High self-esteem can boost your confidence and resilience.
- **Coping skills:** Effective coping skills can help you manage stress and adversity.

Building Resilience:
Building resilience takes time and effort, but it's a worthwhile investment. Here are some strategies for building resilience:
- **Develop a positive mindset:** Cultivate a positive outlook and focus on the bright side of things.
- **Practice mindfulness:** Mindfulness can help you stay calm and focused in the face of adversity.
- **Build strong relationships:** Surround yourself with supportive people who can offer encouragement and advice.
- **Learn from setbacks:** View setbacks as opportunities for growth and learning.
- **Set realistic goals:** Set achievable goals and celebrate your successes, no matter how small.
- **Take care of yourself:** Prioritize self-care by getting enough sleep, eating healthy, and exercising regularly.
- **Seek professional help:** If you're struggling to cope with adversity, consider seeking help from a therapist or counselor.

Coping with Setbacks:

When faced with setbacks, it's important to develop effective coping strategies. Here are some tips for coping with setbacks:

- **Acknowledge your feelings:** It's okay to feel sad, angry, or frustrated. Acknowledge your emotions and allow yourself to process them.
- **Challenge negative thoughts:** Identify and challenge negative thoughts about yourself and the situation.
- **Seek support:** Talk to friends, family, or a mentor for support and encouragement.
- **Take a break:** Sometimes, it's helpful to take a break from the situation to gain perspective.
- **Focus on the positive:** Look for the silver lining in the situation.
- **Learn from your mistakes:** Use setbacks as opportunities to learn and grow.
- **Set new goals:** If you've experienced a setback, set new goals and focus on moving forward.

The Benefits of Resilience:

Resilient individuals are better equipped to handle challenges, overcome obstacles, and achieve their goals. They are also more likely to experience:

- **Increased happiness and well-being:** Resilience is associated with higher levels of happiness and well-being.
- **Improved relationships:** Resilient people are better able to build and maintain strong relationships.
- **Greater success:** Resilience is often associated with greater success in both personal and professional life.

Overcoming Adversity:

Overcoming adversity requires courage, determination, and resilience. By developing these qualities, you can bounce back from setbacks and achieve your goals. Remember, setbacks are a normal part of life. It's how you respond to them that determines your ultimate success.

Additional Tips for Building Resilience:
- **Practice gratitude:** Focus on the positive aspects of your life.
- **Find meaning in your struggles:** Look for lessons or insights that can help you grow.
- **Be patient:** Building resilience takes time. Be patient and persistent.
- **Don't give up:** Even when things get tough, don't give up on your dreams.

By developing resilience, you can overcome adversity and achieve your goals. Remember, setbacks are a normal part of life. It's how you respond to them that determines your ultimate success.

ESSENTIAL SKILLS FOR SELF-DEFENSE

In the competitive world of business, it's essential to be prepared for any situation. One crucial aspect of survival is self-defense. While physical self-defense is important, it's equally important to develop emotional and psychological self-defense skills.

Emotional Self-Defense:
- **Develop emotional intelligence:** Understanding and managing your own emotions, as well as those of others, is crucial for navigating the corporate jungle.
- **Practice mindfulness:** Mindfulness can help you stay calm and focused in stressful situations.
- **Build resilience:** Resilience is the ability to bounce back from setbacks. Develop resilience by building a strong support network, practicing self-care, and cultivating a positive mindset.

- **Set boundaries:** Setting boundaries can help you protect yourself from exploitation and maintain a healthy work-life balance.
- **Learn to say no:** Don't be afraid to say no when you're feeling overwhelmed or overextended.

Psychological Self-Defense:
- **Protect your reputation:** Your reputation is your most valuable asset. Avoid engaging in negative or harmful behaviors that could damage your reputation.
- **Build trust:** Trust is essential for building relationships and succeeding in the corporate world. Be honest, reliable, and trustworthy.
- **Avoid gossip:** Avoid participating in gossip or spreading rumors. Gossip can be harmful and damaging to relationships.
- **Develop a thick skin:** Be prepared to handle criticism and rejection.
- **Stay informed:** Stay up-to-date on industry trends and developments. This will help you anticipate potential threats and challenges.

Physical Self-Defense:
 While physical self-defense is not always necessary, it's essential to have a basic understanding of self-defense techniques. Here are some tips:
- **Take a self-defense class:** Enroll in a self-defense class to learn practical skills and techniques.
- **Be aware of your surroundings:** Be aware of your surroundings and trust your instincts.
- **Avoid dangerous situations:** If possible, avoid situations that could be dangerous.
- **De-escalation techniques:** Learn de-escalation techniques to calm down a tense situation.
- **Know your rights:** Understand your legal rights and when to call for help.

Additional Tips for Self-Defense:
- **Build a support network:** Surround yourself with supportive people who can offer advice and encouragement.
- **Practice self-care:** Take care of your physical and mental health.
- **Develop a strong sense of self-worth:** Believe in yourself and your abilities.
- **Be assertive:** Express your needs and opinions clearly and confidently.
- **Trust your instincts:** If something feels wrong, trust your instincts and take action.

By developing emotional, psychological, and physical self-defense skills, you can protect yourself from harm and thrive in the corporate jungle. Remember, the best defense is often prevention. By being aware of your surroundings, building strong relationships, and taking care of yourself, you can minimize your risk of being a victim.

PART IV

Swimming to the Top

CHAPTER 8
THE SHARK'S PERSPECTIVE

THINKING LIKE A SHARK: ADOPTING A PREDATORY MINDSET

In the competitive world of business, adopting a predatory mindset can give you a significant advantage. Sharks are highly skilled predators with a unique set of strategies and tactics that can be applied to the corporate world. By thinking like a shark, you can become more assertive, confident, and successful.

Understanding the Predatory Mindset:
Sharks are apex predators, meaning they are at the top of the food chain. They have evolved to be highly efficient hunters, capable of adapting to changing conditions and outsmarting their prey. The predatory mindset is characterized by:

- **Focus:** Sharks are laser-focused on their prey. They have a single-minded determination to achieve their goals.
- **Aggression:** Sharks are aggressive hunters. They are not afraid to take risks or use force to achieve their objectives.
- **Adaptability:** Sharks are highly adaptable creatures. They can change their hunting strategies to suit different conditions.
- **Resilience:** Sharks are resilient and persistent. They don't give up easily, even in the face of setbacks.
- **Ruthlessness:** Sharks are ruthless predators. They are not afraid to eliminate competition or exploit opportunities.

Applying the Predatory Mindset to Your Career:

By adopting a predatory mindset, you can become a more effective and successful professional. Here are some strategies for thinking like a shark:

- **Set clear goals:** Identify your goals and develop a plan to achieve them.
- **Be aggressive:** Be assertive and confident in your pursuit of your goals.
- **Be adaptable:** Be willing to change your plans and strategies as needed.
- **Be resilient:** Don't give up easily. Persevere through setbacks and challenges.
- **Be ruthless:** Eliminate competition and seize opportunities.
- **Network strategically:** Build relationships with influential people who can help you achieve your goals.
- **Negotiate effectively:** Learn to negotiate effectively to get the best possible deals.
- **Take calculated risks:** Be willing to take calculated risks to achieve your goals.

Avoiding the Pitfalls:

While adopting a predatory mindset can be beneficial, it's important to avoid the pitfalls. Here are some things to keep in mind:

- **Be ethical:** Avoid unethical or illegal behavior.
- **Be mindful of your relationships:** Don't alienate others with your aggressive behavior.
- **Be realistic:** Set realistic goals and expectations.
- **Don't become a bully:** Avoid bullying or intimidating others.

The Benefits of Thinking Like a Shark:

By adopting a predatory mindset, you can:

- **Increase your confidence:** Thinking like a shark can boost your self-esteem and confidence.

- **Achieve your goals:** A predatory mindset can help you achieve your goals more effectively.
- **Become a leader:** Sharks are natural leaders. By thinking like a shark, you can develop leadership skills.
- **Survive in a competitive environment:** The predatory mindset is essential for survival in the competitive world of business.

Thinking like a shark is not about being ruthless or unethical. It's about adopting a mindset of focus, aggression, adaptability, resilience, and ruthlessness. By applying these principles to your career, you can become a more effective and successful professional.

BECOMING A LEADER: INSPIRING OTHERS TO FOLLOW

In the competitive world of business, leadership is essential for success. Effective leaders are able to inspire and motivate others to achieve common goals. By developing your leadership skills, you can increase your influence, advance your career, and make a positive impact on the world.

Understanding Leadership:
Leadership is the ability to influence others to achieve common goals. It's not about being the boss or having the most authority. True leaders inspire and motivate others to follow them because they believe in their vision and values.

Essential Qualities of a Leader:
Effective leaders possess a variety of qualities, including:
- **Vision:** Leaders have a clear vision of where they want to go and can inspire others to follow.
- **Communication:** Leaders are able to communicate effectively and clearly articulate their vision.

- **Empathy:** Leaders are able to understand and empathize with others.
- **Integrity:** Leaders are honest, trustworthy, and ethical.
- **Resilience:** Leaders are able to bounce back from setbacks and challenges.
- **Decisiveness:** Leaders are able to make difficult decisions and take action.
- **Humility:** Leaders are humble and willing to learn from others.
- **Courage:** Leaders are courageous and willing to take risks.
- **Passion:** Leaders are passionate about their work and can inspire others with their enthusiasm.

Developing Leadership Skills:
Developing leadership skills takes time and effort. Here are some strategies for becoming a more effective leader:
- **Seek out leadership opportunities:** Look for opportunities to take on leadership roles, such as leading a team or project.
- **Develop your communication skills:** Effective communication is essential for leadership.
- **Build relationships:** Build strong relationships with your team members and colleagues.
- **Be a role model:** Lead by example and demonstrate the behaviors you expect from others.
- **Seek feedback:** Ask for feedback from others to identify areas for improvement.
- **Continue learning:** Stay up-to-date on industry trends and developments.
- **Practice empathy:** Try to understand the perspectives of others.
- **Be decisive:** Make decisions promptly and confidently.

- **Be humble:** Be willing to admit your mistakes and learn from them.

Inspiring Others:

To inspire others to follow, leaders must be able to communicate their vision effectively and create a positive and supportive environment. Here are some strategies for inspiring others:

- **Be passionate:** Show your passion for your work and your vision.
- **Be authentic:** Be yourself and be genuine.
- **Empower others:** Empower your team members to take ownership of their work.
- **Recognize and reward achievement:** Recognize and reward the accomplishments of your team members.
- **Create a positive work environment:** Foster a positive and supportive work environment.
- **Lead by example:** Demonstrate the behaviors you expect from others.

Overcoming Challenges:

Leadership can be challenging. Here are some common challenges that leaders face:

- **Resistance to change:** People may resist change, even if it is beneficial.
- **Conflict:** Conflict is a natural part of any organization.
- **Time management:** Leaders must be able to manage their time effectively.
- **Stress:** Leadership can be stressful.

The Benefits of Leadership:

Effective leadership can have a significant impact on an organization's success. Leaders can inspire and motivate others to achieve their goals, improve morale, and create a positive work environment.

How To Swim With The Sharks Without Being Eaten Alive

Becoming a leader requires dedication, hard work, and a commitment to personal and professional development. By developing your leadership skills, you can increase your influence, advance your career, and make a positive impact on the world.

CHAPTER 9
THE LEGACY OF THE SURVIVOR

LEAVING A LASTING IMPACT: MAKING A DIFFERENCE IN THE WORLD

In the competitive world of business, it's easy to get caught up in the pursuit of personal success and financial gain. However, true fulfillment comes from making a positive impact on the world. By leaving a lasting legacy, you can find meaning and purpose in your work.

The Importance of Making a Difference:
Making a difference in the world can have a profound impact on your life. It can give you a sense of purpose, fulfillment, and satisfaction. It can also help you build strong relationships, inspire others, and create a positive legacy.

Identifying Your Passion:
To make a lasting impact, you need to identify your passion. What are you truly passionate about? What drives you? Once you've identified your passion, you can channel your energy and focus toward making a difference.

Finding Your Niche:
Once you've identified your passion, you need to find your niche. What unique skills or experiences do you have that can contribute to making a difference? How can you leverage your talents to create a positive impact?

Setting Goals:
Once you've identified your passion and niche, it's time to set goals. What specific impact do you want to make? What are your short-term and long-term objectives?

Taking Action:

To make a lasting impact, you need to take action. Here are some strategies for making a difference:

- **Volunteer your time:** Volunteer for a cause that you care about.
- **Donate to charities:** Support organizations that are making a positive impact.
- **Start your own nonprofit:** If you have a passion for a particular cause, consider starting your own nonprofit organization.
- **Use your platform:** If you have a platform, such as a blog or social media following, use it to raise awareness and inspire others.
- **Mentor others:** Mentor young people or professionals who are just starting out in their careers.
- **Support sustainable businesses:** Choose to support businesses that are committed to social and environmental responsibility.

Overcoming Challenges:

Making a difference can be challenging. There may be obstacles, setbacks, and sacrifices involved. However, the rewards are well worth the effort.

Measuring Your Impact:

It can be difficult to measure the impact you're making. However, there are ways to track your progress and assess your impact. For example, you can:

- **Collect testimonials:** Ask people who have benefited from your work to share their stories.
- **Track metrics:** Track metrics such as the number of people you've helped or the amount of money you've raised for your cause.
- **Reflect on your journey:** Reflect on your experiences and the positive impact you've made.

Leaving a Lasting Legacy:
Making a lasting impact is about more than just achieving short-term goals. It's about creating a legacy that will be remembered for generations to come. By identifying your passion, setting goals, and taking action, you can make a meaningful difference in the world.

Additional Tips for Making a Lasting Impact:
- **Be patient:** Making a lasting impact takes time and effort. Be patient and persistent.
- **Collaborate with others:** Partner with like-minded individuals to amplify your impact.
- **Be authentic:** Be true to yourself and your values.
- **Celebrate your successes:** Celebrate your achievements, no matter how small.
- **Never give up:** Even in the face of setbacks, never give up on your dream of making a difference.

By leaving a lasting impact, you can find true fulfillment and purpose in your life. Remember, even the smallest actions can have a ripple effect that extends far beyond your own life.

EMBRACING THE JOURNEY: FINDING FULFILLMENT IN THE STRUGGLE

The corporate world can be a challenging and demanding place. It's easy to get caught up in the pursuit of success and forget about the journey itself. However, finding fulfillment in the struggle can be incredibly rewarding.

The Importance of Embracing the Journey:
Embracing the journey means focusing on the process rather than just the outcome. It's about enjoying the challenges and learning from your experiences. When you embrace the journey, you're more likely to:

- **Find meaning and purpose:** The journey can be just as rewarding as the destination.
- **Build resilience:** Overcoming challenges can help you build resilience and perseverance.
- **Develop new skills:** The journey can help you develop new skills and abilities.
- **Create lasting memories:** The experiences you have along the way can create lasting memories.
- **Make a positive impact:** The journey can provide you with opportunities to make a positive impact on the world.

Overcoming Challenges:

The journey is not always easy. There will be setbacks, obstacles, and challenges along the way. However, it's important to remember that these challenges can be valuable learning experiences.

- **Embrace setbacks:** View setbacks as opportunities for growth and learning.
- **Stay focused on your goals:** Keep your eye on the prize and don't get sidetracked by obstacles.
- **Seek support:** Talk to friends, family, or a mentor for support and encouragement.
- **Practice gratitude:** Focus on the positive aspects of your journey.
- **Celebrate your successes:** Celebrate your achievements, no matter how small.

Finding Fulfillment in the Struggle:

Finding fulfillment in the struggle means appreciating the journey and focusing on the process rather than just the outcome. Here are some tips for finding fulfillment:

- **Set meaningful goals:** Set goals that are aligned with your values and passions.
- **Focus on the process:** Enjoy the journey and appreciate the experiences along the way.

- **Learn from your mistakes:** Use setbacks as opportunities to learn and grow.
- **Be patient:** Success takes time. Be patient and persistent.
- **Find meaning in your work:** Look for ways to make a positive impact with your work.
- **Connect with others:** Build strong relationships with people who support and inspire you.
- **Practice mindfulness:** Mindfulness can help you appreciate the present moment and find fulfillment in the journey.

The Benefits of Embracing the Journey:

Embracing the journey can have numerous benefits, including:

- **Increased happiness and well-being:** Focusing on the journey can help you find greater happiness and fulfillment.
- **Improved resilience:** Overcoming challenges can help you build resilience and perseverance.
- **Stronger relationships:** The journey can help you build stronger relationships with others.
- **A sense of purpose:** Finding meaning and purpose in your work can be incredibly rewarding.
- **A lasting legacy:** The experiences you have along the way can help you create a lasting legacy.

Embracing the journey is not about giving up on your goals. It's about finding fulfillment in the process and appreciating the experiences along the way. By focusing on the journey, rather than just the destination, you can find greater meaning and satisfaction in your life.

CONCLUSION

The corporate world can be a treacherous place, filled with sharks and other predators. To survive and thrive in this environment, you must be prepared to adapt, overcome challenges, and develop the skills necessary to succeed.

- **Understand the sharks:** Recognize the different types of sharks and their motivations.
- **Develop shark survival skills:** Build confidence, learn to deceive, and network effectively.
- **Outmaneuver the sharks:** Turn the tables on your predators and take control of the situation.
- **Swim to the top:** Become a leader and make a lasting impact.

The journey to success is not always easy. There will be setbacks, challenges, and obstacles along the way. However, by understanding the corporate jungle and developing the necessary survival tactics, you can overcome adversity and achieve your goals.

Remember, the key to success is not just about surviving. It's about thriving. By embracing the journey, learning from your experiences, and developing your skills, you can not only survive in the corporate jungle, but also make a positive impact on the world.

Made in United States
Orlando, FL
25 November 2024